Faith Like A
CHILD

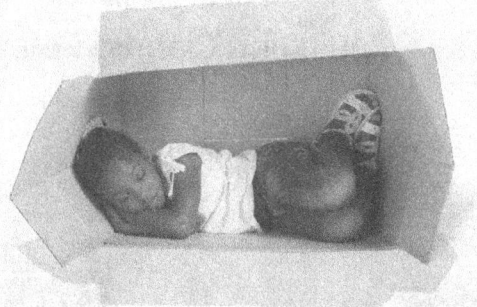

The true life story of a homeless girl encountering
God's miracle through faith

PAULA PENHA
CLAUDIO PENHA

Faith Like A Child

Paula and Claudio Penha

Copyright © 2019 Paula Penha. All Rights Reserved

"Faith Like A Child" is a riveting and honest account of what it means to watch the faithfulness of God protect and provide through every dark season of your life. Proving once again that it's not where you start, but it's how you finish and you'll win if you don't quit.

   --Evangelist Cheryl Boggs

   Radio Host, Recording Artist

The life story recounted in this book is a great testimony of how God heard the cries of a child in deep distress, and gave her family a completely new beginning. Paula's life story tells of one who went from victim to victor, and is an extraordinary example of God's redeeming love. She is a dedicated mother and wife, and has a passion for her Lord that is contagious. In reading this book, you will agree that only God could have turned her life around in such a dramatic way!

   --Pastor Sheila Bowling,

   Eagle Rock Ministries

   Gritty Women of God

In this book you will read of abuse, abandonment, and severe rejection. Satan truly comes to steal, kill and destroy. After repetitive disappointments in life, people, and at times she felt even God, Paula refuses to quit and hangs on. With truly a mustard size seed of faith hidden in her souls, she sees God send a deliverer to help bring her out of the pit of poverty, depression and the insanity of life. All that happened to Paula doesn't identify who she is. Now as daughter of God, she dances and praises the King of Kings and serves Him faithfully. I believe you will be inspired to not quit and to continue on this journey of faith, hope and the pursuit of your destiny as you read this book. Never quit, continue on and give Glory to God.

--Dr. Brian Adams
Author of "The Power of Forgiveness"

DEDICATION

This book is dedicated to my mother, who I watched struggle endlessly to give us the best life she could, and to my husband, whose limitless patience and affectionate devotion taught me what loyalty and commitment really looks like.

CONTENTS

Title..1
Dedication..5
Contents...6
Introduction...7
Chapter 1: Just surviving.......................14
Chapter 2: The Way to Rock Bottom......26
Chapter 3: Pizza Angel............................33
Chapter 4: The Notice.............................50
Chapter 5: The Shelter............................57
Chapter 6: End of My Rope...................68
Chapter 7: The Letter.............................79
Chapter 8: The Heavyweight Champ......91
Chapter 9: but joy comes in the morning..102
Acknowledgements................................109

Introduction

Growing up, the only constant in my life was change. And that typically seems to be the normal with mostly everyone. But everyone's normal is not the same. This story is about a season in my life where I saw the faithfulness of God manifest in such a way that it grounded my faith in Him for the rest of my life.

I was raised by my mom. She was a single mother and she had five children to take care of. She had her first child when she was only seventeen years old, and had her last, me, at the age of twenty-five.

My father, and I say "father" because I didn't get a chance to know him well enough to really understand what it meant to call him "Dad," stuck around just long enough until I reached the age of two. Before me, he got my mom pregnant several other times but he wasn't very good with the follow-through when it came to my siblings and I. there are some recollections I have of him being around when I was a child, but nearly all of the most vivid memories of him and his family I would rather forget. Suffice it to say, I never knew what the phrase "Daddy's little girl" meant, or what it felt like to be one.

I don't have any ill-will towards my father, as hurt as I have always been by his absence. Through the years I tried several times to contact him in an attempt to mend what has always been broken between us, and I was able to salvage the relationship as best I knew how. But more of that later.

My father made his share of mistakes early on in his marriage to my mom. In fact, sadly enough, infidelity was a familiar pain my mom endured while married to him. There was a time when while my mom was pregnant, another woman not too far from our neighborhood was pregnant at the same time, carrying another one of my father's children. Sometimes I wonder if there are other half siblings of mine that I haven't met. If so, I pray that they were able to overcome the lives I imagined they were forced to lead, because I know for me it was a difficult road to travel in the early part of my life.

Not having a dad growing up is hard, really hard—especially for a little girl. And my heart breaks for anyone who has to go through life without ever feeling loved by their own father. But I was lucky in that I had a different kind of father. I had a Heavenly Father. Sometimes, though, I even felt like He had walked out on me.

Yes, there were some dark times in my life—times when I thought that surely God must've forgotten about me. I was only about two when my dad left us once and for all. It's not like things were ever easy when he was around, since he made such a sporadic appearance in our lives. I didn't know when it was the last time he shut the door on his way out of his marriage to my mom and out of my life, but I was soon destined to find out that life was not going to get any easier for me and my family. And I was right about that.

My world went from bad to worse, and I could tell because I saw it all over my mom's face everyday. I think that my father walking out on us the way he did probably cut her deeper than it did any of us. I don't know if it was because she wanted him to stick around for us or because of the sense of betrayal and abandonment she felt, but my father turning his back on us shattered my mom's heart. I don't know that she ever fully recovered—not for a long while, anyway.

Not only did the father of her children leave her high and dry, but my mom's own mother had challenges of her own. Physically she wasn't far from us; we all lived around Columbus, Ohio, but she had a difficult time demonstrating an affectionate love that my mom desperately needed. My mom had raised herself from the time she was fourteen on, so she had been on her own for quite some time. Even before my mom finally left my grandmother's house, she practically was on her own already. There was something missing from my grandmother—something she didn't get that most women did when they had children. It's like her maternal instinct just never turned on. Maybe her mother never showed her any affectionate love so she just didn't know how. Whatever it was that caused it, it kept her from ever fully protecting or loving my mom the way a parent is supposed to.

My mom grew up just like I did, without a dad. My grandmother also worked all the time, just like my mom did, to try to raise a family by herself. And that's all my grandmother thought she needed to do as a parent. She figured that as long as she was going to work, keeping a roof over her kids' heads, and keeping food on the table, her job was done. Perhaps she didn't see the need in being affectionate. She provided the basic provisions and the rest was up to my mom and her siblings.

After feeling detached and emotionally empty for so long, my mom didn't stay around too much longer.

My mom's upbringing trickled down to my siblings and me. Between the stress of my dad coming and going and the fact that she hadn't been loved by anyone in a real way, she had no idea how to show us any affection. I really don't remember my mom just holding me in her arms or tucking me in at night and kissing me on the forehead. I actually can't recall ever really being hugged as a little girl, outside of church anyway.

Church was my haven growing up as a kid, and it is one way that my mom proved to us how much she loved us, by making sure we knew who God was and what Jesus had sacrificed for us. Every

Sunday come Hell or high water, whatever siblings of mine were left in the house, we were loaded on the church bus and taken away to Sunday school. Even when my mom had to work, she was sure to get us out to the church bus by 9 a.m.

She may have had trouble verbally telling us that she loved us, but I knew deep down that her heart beat for us. My mom's dedication to getting us to the Friendship Baptist Church every Sunday morning was her way of wrapping us up in her arms and saying, "This is how much I love you." And I cherished every second I got to spend in church. I loved the people and the meals that were provided after service was over. It was the one day of the week when I felt whole as a person. It was the one day I got to interact with other nice families and I got to worship my heavenly Father. Plus, the big meals after church never hurt either and all the people who weren't afraid to hug or say, "I love you, child. And so does Jesus!"

Even though I wasn't quite sure how to return that love to the people in my congregation, I liked how it felt. And no matter how awkward I was or how much I recoiled into myself when someone went to hug me, the members of my church just kept on because they had the love of God, and they didn't need me to return the affection to keep on loving me. I was always a little introverted because of my rejection issues, so I never got too close to people in the church, but just gathering with others, the love, and God was enough to make me feel like I was a part of something. And my mom was sure to send me there so I could feel that great feeling of love and belonging as well as get my spiritual nourishment. I love my mom for that.

That is why I never felt upset with my mom for not being able to hug us and snuggle with us like other moms did. And that is why, when our lives began to fall apart completely, my heart broke not for only for me, but for my mother. And our lives certainly did fall apart. We were just barely hanging on to keep ourselves from rock bottom, but finally the threads that kept us up snapped right in two. And we fell hard.

Chapter One: Just Surviving

By the year of 1990, it was only my brother Paul and I left in the house with our mom. My other brothers and sisters had already moved on, so that left Paul and I to fend for ourselves most of the time. My mom was working as a nurse's aid, cleaning up after old folks in nursing homes, almost around the clock just to keep a roof over our heads, so Paul and I spent a lot of time on our own.

By the time we were in junior high, my dad was long gone. He didn't even bother to check in any more. That meant that my mom was responsible for us in every way and she didn't get help from anyone. My grandmother was only about fifteen minutes from us, but she wasn't involved in our lives like she could have been. Like my dad, she was hardly ever around. That was just her way though. And at least with her, there was no dramatic ending the way there was with my father.

I remember very well the day my dad decided to walk out on us for good. Some things you don't forget even if you wish you could. What I remember most about the day wasn't how I felt though. It was how Paul looked. I didn't know it then because I was only six, but I saw someone break for the first time in my life that day. I saw something leave Paul that I'm not sure he ever got back.

My father didn't seem to feel comfortable in a dad skin—not with me and my siblings, anyway. Although he committed in marrying my mom and in getting her pregnant, it was tragic that he didn't commit to raising us. Perhaps it was because he himself was not raised by his father. My belief is that he didn't know how to be a dad at that phase of his life. In many areas of my life, responsibility didn't fall under a strong suite for my dad when it involved me.

When I was only six years old, that would have made Paul eight, my dad put the last nail in the coffin, so to speak. He had left my mom once again.

Anyway, one day Paul and I were out in front of the house playing when my dad rolled up with his new girlfriend. I guess he was probably there to get whatever stuff he had left at our house. I don't know for sure because he was very deliberate in avoiding Paul and me. I had come to the conclusion, even as young as six, that I would rather be with my mom than my dad, so I didn't take much notice of what he was doing. There were parts of me, like there are of every little girl, that desperately wanted my dad to love me, but the bigger part of me was uneasy about being with him.

The reason I had such ambivalent feelings for my father was that just two years before that day he came cruising by with a teenage lover, I had been molested in the basement of his sister's house. It wasn't by my dad. It was by two of my male cousins.

It was a Sunday and I imagine my mom was working a weekend shift, as she was prone to do. My dad took us over to my aunt's house for Sunday lunch. As soon as we got there, my two cousins, one of which was eighteen and the other nineteen at the time, called me down to the basement to see puppies. I loved animals, so I was thrilled to get to play with a bunch of fuzzy, newborn dogs. But that was not what I found when I got to the bottom of the basement steps.

"Come on Paula," one of my cousins said, with his pants undone. I could see from where I stood that they were both exposing themselves to me.

"No," I said in a whisper, backing toward the stairs.

"You better or that dog is gonna eat you up," the other cousin said. "If you make a sound that dog will rip you to shreds, little girl," he warned.

"All we have to do is tell him to get you, so you better keep your mouth shut," the older of the two added.

I was four and I was terrified. I looked down at the dog—it was a big dog, a pit bull mix or something like that. I pictured it chewing up my arms and gnawing on my legs. I didn't want that dog to kill me right there in the basement, so I stayed perfectly quiet. And while I stayed silent, my cousins made it so that I would not be able to trust a man for years and years to come. That day as my dad sat above me in the kitchen, talking away, my cousins stole my innocence and my ability to feel safe around a man. And I never told a soul because they made it clear I wouldn't like what would happen if I did. I think back and wonder if I had the courage to tell my dad if the outcome would have been different. I know he would have done something about it. I just didn't feel comfortable telling him, even if I hadn't been threatened not to tell.

That was how I saw my dad, as not close enough to tell something to. So to me, him showing up with a little girlfriend was not as traumatizing as it was for Paul. See, Paul still looked up to him. That was Paul's dad—his role model. Paul was only eight, and when you are an eight-year-old boy, your dad is World's Greatest Dad no matter what he does. A boy's dad is his life. It is who he wants to impress and who he wants to be when he grows up.

Whether he deserved it or not, Paul gave my dad a lot of credit, and he also loved him with all his eight-year-old heart. So when my dad just got in the car and drove off that evening, Paul went into hysterics. His dad, the one man he wanted to love him more than anyone else in the world, left him in a cloud of exhaust and didn't even look back. My brother wasn't going to let him off so easy, though.

"Daddy! Daddy, wait!" Paul screamed after the car as he ran off into the streets, barefoot and covered in dirt from playing outside all day. "Daddy!" he bellowed with giant tears rolling down his dirty face. "Please!"

I stood in the yard and watched. It was the first time I felt my heart actually hurt. Watching my brother chase after that old Buick, I felt my heart break right into two pieces. I think it was the youngest heartbreak ever.

Paul, on the other hand, just planted himself at the side of the road. His eyes stayed locked on the backend of the car as my father disappeared out of our lives for good. We were half-orphaned that day and Paul's Superman was dead. He'd have to find himself a new man to look up to.

One day Paul and my other brother Norman were out and about and they happened to run into my father and his girlfriend. They ran to the car and asked him, "Daddy, when are you going to come see us?".

He responded, "I have a new family now."

For boys living in the kind of neighborhood we did where you had to sleep on the floors at night because a stray bullet might find its way into your bedroom, role models were not an easy thing to come by. My dad's presence at least made us feel like we were worth hanging around for, and he gave Paul at the very least an imaginary sense of manhood to work toward. With him gone, Paul had street thugs and gangsters to help mold him as a man. Those don't give a kid very good odds for success, even when they have amazing, little hearts. And my brother Paul had the best heart I'd ever seen.

With my dad gone and my mom working all the time, Paul became my protector. That day when he was left sobbing on the side of the road broke him in some ways, but it also made him strong, for me. I don't know if he made a conscious decision to become the man of the house or if he just kind of fell into the role by force, but however it came to pass, Paul definitely took over as my guardian. Over the next years, he would walk me home so no one tried to mess with me, he would teach me some tricks so we could eat at night, and he would make sure that all the boys around knew beyond a shadow of a doubt that they were not to touch me in any way what-so-ever. I don't know how or what I'd be today if it hadn't been for Paul. I also don't know if he has ever understood what a significant role he played in my life. If he doesn't, I only hope that one day he will, because I know that Paul was a gift to me from God, whether he can say that now or not.

Paul was a good kid, a real good kid, but the threat of starving and living always in want can drive a kid to do things that aren't necessarily morally sound. By the time he was in his early teens, we were going to a school in which the students were slinging drugs and people we knew were being shot in drive-bys. Kids were murdering kids for pot or revenge or money. Walking down to the corner store was like walking through a war zone, and the older you got the more pressures there were on you to pick a crowd to fall into.

A dearth of necessities, whether it is money, food, or just plain safety, can be the breeding ground for wrong-doing. People don't realize how easy it is to justify doing certain things that you never imagined you would do when your stomach is growling. For Paul, he knew that one way or another, we were going to have to find some way to get food. He watched what he saw other people around doing to get what they needed and he taught me how to do what we had to do to get by.

We got food stamps to help supplement my mom's limited income, but most of the time we had to find creative ways to use that money to keep the lights on and the water running.

Back in those days, there weren't such a thing as an EBT card. Food stamps was just that, big stamps that looked like monopoly money and that is where the creativity kicked in.

"I need you all to take these stamps and buy a pack of gum and bring me home the change. Each of you do that at as many places you can or we won't have any lights," my mom would tell us when we'd get a cut-off notice in the mail. She was working herself sick, but still she only made enough to pay rent every month, and sometimes she couldn't even do that.

Because my mom's income was never quite enough, I had become very familiar with eviction notices. Most of the time they were printed on bright colored paper—red mostly. When I'd see a red or yellow or bright orange piece of paper stuck to the door, I'd know it was time to pack up our stuff and get ready to move. We usually got a first warning that gave us a couple of weeks, and then when the second showed up it was time to go.

When we'd get kicked out, Mom would dart around town looking for any low-rent place that let you in without doing a credit check or asking for references. That meant we were always in the worst parts of town and we were usually renting from slumlords who never kept anything working right in a house because they knew the tenants had no other choice. It seems like when you're broke, you lose some basic human rights. I know that we were seldom treated the same as the middleclass. The slumlords, the electric companies, the store owners kicking us out for fear we'd take something—they didn't see us as people anymore. We were a way to earn a quick buck, a resident who didn't deserve to have lights, or a drain on net profits. We were hardly ever just people who needed a little help, though. It's hard for some folks to recover after spending their lives as second-rate. And it's sad that there is such a divide in humanity, but if my childhood taught me anything, it was that there was definitely a divide between the rich and poor, or even the middleclass and the poor.

So while my mom slaved away cleaning bedpans, Paul and I made trips back and forth to the surrounding convenient stores to buy something that only cost a quarter so we could use our food stamps to keep the lights on, which meant that we weren't using the food stamps to buy food. That kept us always searching for creative ways to get a meal. If we couldn't find a way to eat, we would have to use our food stamps for food; and if we used our food stamps for food, that meant at times we wouldn't be able to pay the light bill or the water bill. So, if we did have full stomachs, we had to do our homework by candlelight because sometimes there wasn't enough to pay the bills and eat. We also had the water turned off on several occasions, so we couldn't brush our teeth or take baths until we either moved or somehow scrounged enough money to pay the bill.

We would rely sometimes on neighbors to let us use their toilet or take a quick shower and neither Paul nor I had any idea what a new pair of jeans or tennis shoes were. We got hand-me-downs from neighbors or people from the church, garage sale specials, or thrift store outfits that cost us maybe a couple of quarters, a dollar at most. Finding a pair of shoes that were my size and not too scuffed up was like Christmas morning for me. Instead of a new bike or a video game system, I just wanted to wear something that no one else had. I wanted to have something that hadn't been worn out by a stranger already and tossed out in the "give away" pile. But when you can barely afford to eat, those kinds of things are as far away as owning a yacht.

    I tried to be thankful for all the little things, but it seemed that little by little, we didn't even have little things to be thankful for. And the older I got, the harder it was to see my mom in so much agony over everything that she couldn't provide for us. I just knew every time we got a shutoff notice and every time there was a red piece of paper taped to our door that my mom was going to break. And sure enough, there were times that she did.

Chapter Two: The Way to Rock Bottom

I don't know that I remember my mom's very first mental breakdown, but I do know that the first one came when I was young, and they continued for years. My mom lived a tough life and she always felt like she wasn't doing enough for her children. The funny thing was, I saw what she did and I knew for a fact that she was working herself sick for us.

Even though she had no one to help her and she could hardly ever make ends meet, my mom still put every extra penny she came by toward getting a little something special for us. It wasn't often that there was anything at all left over, but if for some odd reason there was, my mom used that money on us. I know that if she had it, we would have been spoiled. I also knew that it wasn't her fault that we struggled. Unfortunately, my mom couldn't see that, so she always beat herself down for not being able to give us everything she wanted to.

My mom never spent anything on herself. All she wanted in the world was to give Paul and me a good life. But no matter how many hours she worked or how hard she tried, the bills and expenses seemed to outweigh the income. I sometimes think that my mom wanted to buy us toys and new clothes more than we even wanted them ourselves. And the fact the she couldn't give us those things drove her into a deep despair, to the point of hospitalization.

I can remember one afternoon when I was just about ten or so that I saw my mom hit what I thought at the time was rock bottom. I don't remember what the cause was—I imagine a cut-off notice or a red slip on the door. Whatever it was, it sent my mom into an episode. Before I knew it, there was an ambulance outside our house and paramedics coming in toting a stretcher.

"Where's your mom, sweetie?" one of the men dressed all in blue wearing latex gloves asked me. I pointed to my mom's bedroom.

They went into where my mom was and loaded her on the metal gurney that was covered in rough, white hospital sheets. I stood quietly in the hallway, trying my best to stay out of the way as the paramedics strapped an oxygen mask on my mom's face and wheeled her out to the ambulance. I stayed still and quiet until I saw the ambulance door slam closed and my mom disappear behind the orange and white door.

"Momma!" I screamed out as the ambulance lurched forward. "Momma, wait! Don't leave me, Momma! Let me come with you! Please, don't take my mom away!" I bawled as I chased after the ambulance.

I ran down the street calling out for my mom until my legs and lungs burned and my eyes went blurry from all the tears. Like Paul had done so many years before trying to chase our dad down, I eventually admitted defeat and collapsed at the side of the road. I sat crumbled into myself on the hot asphalt, sobbing and wiping the snot and tears from my face. I didn't feel the heat of the blacktop on my skin or notice the oil spills I had landed in. I just wailed and watched as the ambulance disappeared off in the distance. It seemed like we were getting left over and over again as kids. But at least I knew that my mom would be back. I knew that she didn't want to leave us and that it was her love for us that broke her heart so badly that she had a breakdown. That killed me.

Even though it took a breakdown to get her there and she hated knowing that her kids were out on their own, she at very least could get a good three meals a day and enjoy the hot water, the nice cool air, and TV. To someone who was trading their food stamps off to pay the water bill, the hospital might as well be the Ritz-Carlton.

Paul and I would be left to be the adults of the house during the short stints my mom spent in the hospital recovering from a breakdown. Even with my mom stuck in a hospital bed, my dad didn't show his face or offer to help out in any way.

When I saw my mom hauled off, it felt like a piece of me died. There was nothing in the world I hated more than seeing the woman I loved more than anything in so much pain. It didn't seem fair to me that she had to live like that, especially with my dad off doing whatever it was he wanted to do. I also felt sad and guilty because I wanted to be the support in her life. I had seen the tears and saw how much she wanted to provide when she just couldn't. That sadness would eventually turn into anger toward my dad. I couldn't forgive him for just leaving us that way-for just abandoning us and not caring. I struggled not to hate him sometimes when I was just a little girl. Unforgiveness is one the devil's craftiest methods to keep us in bondage. It eats away at your capacity to love slowly but cunningly. And the longer you harbor it, the worst it gets. I'm past that now, but it was a real thorn in my side when I was growing up. That in itself was a journey for me to walk at an early age.

How many of us have had to make a conscious decision to forgive those who offend, hurt or betray us? It is not easy but oh it is so necessary and liberating.

One of the main reasons that I had so much trouble forgiving my dad was the way he could leave my mom so vulnerable. Even when my mom wasn't being hauled off by an ambulance, she was still always struggling—struggling with the bills, struggling with supporting us, struggling with life in general. Leaving my mom was bad enough, but leaving my siblings and I was extremely difficult, confusing and painful.

I would hear my mom crying so many nights and I would just pray to God to help me somehow provide for my family since I knew that no one else was going to. I was only a kid, but I wanted so badly to raise us up out of where we were. I didn't know how I could do it, but I prayed and prayed that God would use me to get us out of there and give us a new life—a happy life where we didn't have to hang our heads down in shame.

It seemed like for some time, God must have been turning a deaf ear to me, because the more I prayed, the worse things got. It was like I had stepped into Job's shoes all of a sudden and every little thing in my life was being taken away from me. Job was the man in the Bible who had some extreme tests in his life where he lost everything that was dear to him. In his story, the outcome ended up being one of blessing beyond his imagination. I had yet to await my blessing from my heavenly Father. I would get really frustrated with God and even angry. But then every once in a while, an angel would pop up out of nowhere to remind me that God was still up there listening to me and looking down on me. And these angels came in the strangest forms—like in the form of a chain restaurant manager, for instance.

Chapter Three: Pizza Angel

I said that Paul and I were the adults of the house when my mom had to be hospitalized, but even when she wasn't on the first floor of the county hospital, my brother and I were somewhat on our own because of my mom's work schedule. As much as she wanted to be there with us, it just wasn't an option because she had to work. She couldn't be in two places at once, so we were left to our own devices much of the time. Without having my mother at home, we were left in a vulnerable position to look for ways to take care of ourselves. That is what led us to shoplifting, but sometimes we had more serendipitous experiences while we were out looking for ways to eat.

One day Paul and I were kicking around town trying to come up with some way to get dinner that night. We had no more food stamps left and no food at home, so we were going to have to go hungry or be really creative. As we walked along the sidewalk, the smell of dough baking caught our attention.

We were starving and had no money, but we decided to stop in at a Domino's we were passing. I don't know what our plans were exactly, because we didn't have a dollar between the two of us. Something drew us in there though, so we turned off the sidewalk and trekked up to the square brick building. Paul pushed the glass door open and I dutifully followed. We walked in and just plopped down at one of the tables near the register. I saw one of the employees, a guy with a button-down shirt and a tie on that was covered up mostly by an apron, look up and smile at us. I blushed and looked away.

"Do you kids want to learn how to make a pizza?" the man asked from behind the counter. Now that I was looking right at him, I could see on his name tag that he was the manager.

Paul and I looked at each other and then stared at the man. We both knew we had nothing better to do, and the man seemed nice enough. Paul shrugged to indicate he was down with the idea. We both slid out of our chairs and joined the manager, who was covered in flour and had pizza crust dough stuck to his hands. He held out two aprons, one for each of us, and pointed us to the sink so we could wash our hands first.

"Come on over here," he said to us as we finished drying our hands and walked back into the kitchen.

I had never been in a restaurant's kitchen before, so I gazed around at all the massive, shining ovens and the stacks and stacks of ingredients that lined the walls. I'd never seen so much food in one place. It was like I'd stumbled into a dream—a delicious dream.

In true form, Paul was eager to talk and chatting up a storm with the manager. I, on the other hand, stayed a little standoffish in the beginning. He seemed like a decent man, but I hadn't had many good experiences with men at that point in my life, so I was still a little leery. Paul had no problems at all telling the Domino's manager all about our lives though. At first, I didn't know if that was such a good idea, but in the long-run I was beyond grateful for Paul's sociability.

"My name is Mike," he told us as he showed us how to get the dough just right.

"I'm Paul and this is my kid sister, Paula," my brother told him.

"Well it's nice to meet you guys," he smiled. "You ready to make this pizza?"

"Oh yeah!" Paul said as he stepped up to the pizza dough.

Mike showed us how to spread the sauce on and then let us pick out whatever ingredients we wanted. Paul piled on the cheeses and the pepperoni. I stood back most of the time and just watched. When we finished the pizza up that day, the manager let us eat our culinary creation.

"It's all yours," he told us. "Let's see if you're any good as pizza chefs."

"Are you for real?" Paul asked.

"You bet," he told him. "You made it, you eat it."

"Aw man," Paul said. "We were starving too! Thanks so much! This is our lucky day!"

"Eat up!" Mike said as he slid the pizza with its hot, bubbling cheese between the two of us at the table.

We hardly ever got to eat pizza, so it tasted like a gourmet meal to my brother and me. Once we had devoured the entire thing and slurped down all the soda our stomachs could hold, the manager said something I was not accustomed to hearing store managers say to us.

"You come back whenever you want and we'll be sure you get something to eat," he said as we were about to leave.

I was floored. I was so used to having cashiers and managers give me the eye when I walked in, to people telling me to leave if I wasn't going to buy anything, and being kicked out of places and asked not to return that I almost couldn't believe my ears. Not only did this man not care that we weren't going to buy anything, but he was willing to just give us something to eat. And on top of that, he gave us an open invitation! I saw God that day in Domino's pizza. To me, it was as miraculous as when the apostles fed all those people with a couple of fish and a few loaves of bread.

For the next three months, everyday that we were able to Paul and I stopped in at the Domino's and everyday, true to his word, we got all the pizza we could eat. On the days that we didn't go to the restaurant, Mike would send out one of his drivers to our house to deliver a pizza to us. In all Paul's chattiness, the store manager had learned everything about us, including our home address.

Our place of residence wasn't the only thing the store manager remembered about us. He also remembered my birthday. I guess either Paul or I had mentioned that my birthday was coming up, and Mike must have gone and written it down as soon as we left, or he had an excellent memory. Either way, he made my twelfth birthday one to remember.

The day of my birthday, I was feeling pretty low. I knew that there would be no birthday party, no cake and ice cream, and no wrapped Barbie doll or new sweater. I also knew that my mom wanted to be able to give me all that, but couldn't, and I didn't blame her for that. No matter whose fault it was or wasn't though, it stings pretty badly to have your birthday come and go without anything special to recognize it. I never had a birthday party or a cake shaped like a butterfly, but I knew that most kids did, and a part of me really wanted that—at least just once in my life.

The evening of my birthday Paul and I were at home alone as usual. We were messing around outside when we saw a ratty old Accord pull up with one of those triangular, plastic Domino's delivery signs strapped to the top of it. We knew that the pizza was for us so we ran to the house to greet the delivery man.

"I heard it was your birthday," the delivery guy said to me. I just blushed and nodded. "Happy birthday!" he said as he handed me the pizza, and then he walked off back to his car.

When we got the pizza in to the kitchen, we pulled the cardboard lid up to see what kind of pizza Mike had sent us that day. When I saw what was in the box, I almost cried. Mike had sent a pepperoni pizza that day, but this pizza was a little different. He had made a happy face out of the pepperonis just for me for my birthday. Looking down at the smiling pizza, I thought that was better than any princess cake or surprise party ever could be. That day when my birthday could have been a very empty and sad one, a Domino's manager made my day a memorable one and it sparked a gratitude in my heart to know God was still looking over us.

The benevolence that the staff at Domino's showed to us demonstrated to Paul and me that there were still good people in the world and that some people still did care.

But as helpful as getting a pizza everyday was, it still wasn't the answer to all our life's problems. Pizza is an amazing food, but it doesn't cure poverty or fill in the gap between the classes.

The pizzas helped feed us before bed, but we still had two other meals and a lot of other needs to worry about. We had to have socks and underwear, shoes (preferably that fit and didn't come from the previous decade), and needed things like toothbrushes and toothpaste. When we didn't even have enough to eat, those kinds of things were out of the question, unless we stole them. I am not proud to say it, but that is eventually what Paul and I had to do. When we had to forgo grocery shopping to keep the water running or the rent paid, Paul started to teach me to steal so we could eat or have things like shampoo and soap.

"You gotta wear a coat, and the bigger the coat, the easier it's gonna be," Paul explained one day as we stood outside a little grocery store. "And you just slip it right up the arm of your coat and act like nothing."

I didn't like the idea of stealing at all. I had been in Sunday school every week since I could remember, and I had a lot of respect for what Jesus and the apostles had to tell us. I knew that I was supposed to do unto others as I would have them do unto me, but I was also tired of going to bed with my stomach rumbling and I already got made fun of for the way my clothes looked, so I didn't want to go without brushing my teeth or using soap too. As I sat and fought with myself about what to do, I remembered Proverbs 6:30, "People do not despise a thief if he steals to satisfy his hunger when he is starving." And we were definitely starving.

When I finally convinced myself that we had no other choice, I followed Paul's lead and I started to steal, keeping that verse from Proverbs close to me the whole time. I also found a way to turn a profit from the gumballs they had sitting up on the counter at a local market. You were supposed to put in a nickel for a gumball sample—that was so you could taste the different flavors before you bought a whole bag. The thing worked on the honor system. I realized that I could switch out a nickel for a penny, and get quite a few gumballs and it would look like I was paying for them. Then I would take the gumballs to school and sell them for a quarter.

Once I had sold off all my gumballs for a sizeable profit, I'd take whatever money I made and my brother and I could eat the salad bar at the Wendy's down the street from our house for $3.99. We'd also pocket as many lemons and sugar packets as we could while we were at the fast-food restaurant so we could make lemonade when we got home. I was glad that none of the employees ever asked us what we were doing with all the lemons.

One day when I was in running my little gumball scheme, the manager of the store had come up on me. He must have been watching me come in day after day, or just noticed me that day. Whatever it was, he saw me drop in a penny and made a beeline for me. I saw him out of the corner of my eye and I immediately knew that I was in trouble.

"How much did you just put in there?" he demanded as he stood over me and the box of gumballs.

I couldn't get myself to say anything. I was too ashamed to tell him what I was doing and I wasn't going to lie to his face and add that to my list of sins for the day. I just kept quiet and stared up at the man, my brown eyes wide and filled with fear and shame. I prayed that he would let me off this time. Thankfully he did, but not without a consequence.

"Just leave the store," he told me. "And I don't want to see you in here again."

I nodded my head and ran out. That was the end of that scam. From that point on my only choice was to straight shoplift and steal. We couldn't even afford to buy anything from the thrift stores sometimes, so we'd have to shoplift clothes—socks and underwear, things that most people take for granted. We'd also have to slip hair brushes and bars of soap into the sleeves of our jackets and hope that no one noticed. I knew that stealing wasn't right and I hated to do it, but we weren't lifting gold watches and Air Jordan's here; we were taking common toiletries and cotton briefs. That went on for a few months and I thought we were as low as low could get. But every time I thought that things couldn't possibly get any worse than they were, it seemed that life was there to prove me wrong.

"I got bad news," my mom said to Paul and me when we got home from school one day. My brother and I had heard a lot of bad news in our lives at that point, so this day was not unlike so many others. Or at least that is what we thought at first.

"I lost my job today," my mom told us and her voice cracked as she said it. I could tell by her puffed up, reddened eyes that she had been crying all day.

"I'm so sorry, Momma," I told her as we all sat staring out into space. "What are we going to do?"

"I don't know," she cried. "I just don't know. I don't know how much more of this I can take."

"It'll be okay," I told her. "We'll get through this somehow. We'll get through this, Momma."

Those were the only words I could think that might help. I wanted to say more, to comfort her and make her stop crying, but there was not much more to do or say at that point. We weren't the kind of family that hugged or laid a hand on another person to console them, so all I could do was sit and stare at my mom as she sobbed in the living room. I knew that I didn't have the words for her, so I just prayed as hard as I could. I talked to God and asked Him what was going on and pleaded with him. By that time in my life my prayers were getting angrier and more desperate.

I had spent plenty of time in church by then and I had heard the pastor and everyone else say how much God loved me and how good I was in God's eyes. Nothing that was happening in my life was lining up with that idea though. If God thought I was so great, why was he just leaving me high and dry all the time? Did I fall short of what he was expecting? Did he not think that we were worth saving? I thought that surely, I or my mom, or someone, had done something to bring this on ourselves since we had one thing after the next go wrong in our lives. None of it made any sense to me.

When my mom lost her job, I finally said to God, "I need you to show me that you are there, God. I need to see that you are a faithful God and that you are there. Lord, where are you? I'm reading your word. I'm living life to the best of my ability. What are you waiting on?"

I was tired of sitting there waiting and listening to my mom cry. I needed God to step up and be faithful to His word. I was just like old Job. I had run out of patience and I needed something to happen. I needed an answer.

"What else needs to happen?" I asked God as I prayed out loud. "What else can I handle? Take this, God, or just take me."

I was the story of Job. My family was the story of Job. We had lost my father, lost one house after the next, lost electricity, lost water, lost a chance at life, and now my mom had lost the one thing keeping us going—her job. Just like Job, I was fed up and if God wasn't going to take my affliction, I wanted off the bus. I did start to curse the day I was born.

Like most of Job's friends, I wondered what I did to deserve all this. You remember how all but one of Job's friends came in and said, "What did you do, Job? You had to have done something to make God so angry," as Job sat around covered in boils after his home, livestock, and family had all been taken from him? That's what I started to feel like; like I must have done something to bring all this on my head. I had no idea what it could have been though. I was a kid—a twelve-year-old girl! What does a twelve-year-old do to deserve all that?

I had been moved around more times than I could count. I got made fun of by everyone at school for my ratty clothes and because I had to eat the free lunches. And every night I had to worry about whether or not I was going to get to eat. I'd had all I could take, and I was not even a teenager yet. I felt the burdens of a seventy-year-old, and I didn't even have a driver's permit.

With so much going on at home and feeling like a constant outcast at school, I started to get depressed. I started to feel hopeless. At school I was made fun of by everyone and I didn't have a single friend other than my own brother, and at home I had to go over to the neighbor's if I needed to use the bathroom because we usually had no running water. I couldn't concentrate on anything but survival anymore, eating and keeping warm when it was cold and cool when it was hot. School started to slip to the background. My education was muted out, overpowered by the noise of my needs. History and algebra and physical science don't mean anything to you when you are too hungry to think and worried about how you're going to get your next meal. And with my mom's job gone, we may have even less, and we hardly had a thing as it was.

Paul was strong-willed and outgoing, so he seemed to handle things a little bit better than I did. I knew that everything got to him, but he didn't seem to withdraw the way I did. His schoolwork was undoubtedly taking a hit, just like mine, but he was a little better about keeping his head up. He was still extroverted and got along okay at school, socially anyway. The thing about Paul, though, was that he put on false airs so people wouldn't see how much he was going through. Where I got quiet and retreated, I think Paul tried to fight back by acting like everything was okay. Everything was not okay though, not by a long shot, and we had only hit the iceberg at that point.

There was a much bigger blow headed our way; something that would make everything else we had gone through seem like just a little bump in the road. Doing homework by candlelight and skipping showers because there was no hot water seemed to me about as bad as it could get. Then when my mom lost her job, I was sure that we couldn't sink any lower than that, but I found out that there was one more level that we hadn't hit yet—one more rung to fall down before we were at our lowest. And when that rung snapped, I knew for sure that God wasn't listening to anything I said anymore.

Chapter Four: The Notice

I got home from school one afternoon and I saw on our door what I had been dreading since my mom told us that she had been laid off from her job. It was that ominous red letter, and I knew exactly what that letter said. It said that we had fourteen days to vacate the premises, and after that the locks would be changed, we would officially be trespassers and all our possessions left in the house would belong to the landlord.

Here we go again, I thought as I walked up and grabbed that menacing slip from our front door. *What's next?* I wondered as I looked at the paper in my hands. *Where do we go from here?*

The minute my mom was laid off from her nurse's aid job, she went crazy looking for another job. She scoured the classified ads and went around looking for "NOW HIRING" signs in windows of businesses and posted on marquees. She had no luck though. My mom hadn't been able to finish high school because she had my sister so young, and that seemed to haunt her when it was time to find a new job. She had worn herself out looking for someone to hire her, but to no avail. Not a single restaurant or business offered her a job and so our eviction was immanent. We were sitting on a ticking time bomb, and finally that bomb went off.

I walked in and put the eviction notice on the kitchen counter so my mom would be able to see it when she came into the room, and then I sat and waited. I was in no rush to crush my mom's spirits anymore than they already had been. We all knew that this was coming because we had already received our first warning. But still, when you get that final eviction notice, it feels like a punch to the guts. I didn't want to be the one to deliver the punch to my own mother, so I thought I'd wait for her to see it. And soon enough she did.

When my mom saw the piece of paper sitting on the counter, she just grabbed her face, collapsed into a chair and said "I don't know how much more I can take. I'm just tired."

"Mom it's gonna be okay. God is going to get us through this. He is going to work it out," I told her, trying to console her.

Even if I didn't quite understand what God was doing at the time, deep down I kept my faith and believed. I was getting frustrated and impatient, but still I believed, and I told my mom what I truly felt in my heart: that God would take care of us.

I don't know what my mom believed at that moment. She just stayed quiet, shook her head, and cried. I am sure that she wanted to trust that everything was going to work out, but with no job and a letter saying that you have to leave your home, it's not easy to trust in anything. We were in a worse place now than we had ever been before in our lives.

When my mom was working, we would just pack up and find a new place—somewhere that was even worse than the place before, with more rats, more bullets, more police sirens and less room. We'd gather all our belongings and go on to another crummy neighborhood and find another crummy apartment. We would use my mom's last paycheck to start back over. This time, though, there was no paycheck. Even the crummiest place in Ohio wouldn't take us now. Slumlords don't care about your credit or your references, but they do care a lot about your deposit, and we didn't have a dime to our names.

"We better enjoy these next two weeks," my mom told us, "because I don't know where we can go from here but the shelter."

"The shelter?" I asked. We had been in a lot of rundown apartments and lived in the worst parts of Columbus, but we had *never* had to live in a shelter before. That wasn't anything that was even on my radar. We couldn't live in a shelter. Even though I had lived life taking gumballs and selling them to make enough money just to eat dinner; even though I had been forced to steal underwear from discount stores; even though I was used to all the kids at school calling me out for my thrift store sneakers, I was still blown away by the thought of being homeless. *Homeless.*

I couldn't be homeless. Old drunks and drug addicts were homeless, not twelve-year-old girls who went to church every Sunday and prayed to God every night. This just didn't make any sense at all.

Okay, God," I said. "I don't have a dad, I don't have friends or toys or clothes, but you cannot do this to me. You cannot let me go live in a shelter. It's time you do something or let me die!"

Two weeks went by and on the fourteenth day we gathered up all we had into a few plastic bags—it was just our clothes, a couple of pairs of socks, a couple of pairs of jeans, and a few shirts each—and we made our way to the nearest shelter. We had to leave the little furniture we had because we didn't have anywhere to store it. But because we never had any money, Paul and I didn't have any toys or stuffed animals to take along or have to leave behind. We didn't have to fret over leaving our T.V. or mess with hauling around a stereo or all our art supplies. We had clothes and that was it. We didn't even have toiletries to take along.

So, we loaded up our few worldly possessions and started walking. In about an hour we arrived on the doorstep of the local shelter. As we stood in front of the shabby, red brick building with boarded up windows, I felt bad for my brother and I, but I felt even worse for my mom. She had tried her best to take care of us but it was just too much, so there we were, homeless and going to the place where all the other folks in the area who had lost it all go. Walking into a shelter is a very strange feeling. Crossing the threshold with your only possessions tossed in a plastic bag feels like the ultimate defeat.

I remember looking around once we got into the shelter and noticing the wide range of people that were there. There were families, old people, young people, and people of all races and nationalities. Even though I was in the same place as all these people, I immediately felt an overwhelming sense of compassion for each and every one of them. My heart ached for them. I forgot all about Paula for a moment and all I wanted to do was to help every person laid out on a cot or tucked away at a table in the back corner. I wanted to tell them all that everything was going to be okay, and I wanted to mean it. I wanted to fix all their problems and give them the life that they deserved.

It was a humbling experience to see so many others at such a low point in their lives. I knew that some of those people had been regulars in that shelter for years and years—some of the children were probably born into that lifestyle. As hard as it was, walking into that shelter made me feel a deep appreciation for the little bit that I had. That feeling waned with time, but for that brief moment when I first arrived at the local shelter, I saw all the blessings in my life and I wanted to share them with every person in there.

Chapter Five: The Shelter

When my mom first told us about the shelter, I had a completely different idea about what the shelter was. Because it is referred to as "the" shelter, I assumed that there was one place that we would be staying until my mom was able to find a job and we could get back to our own place. That wasn't how it worked though.

What really happens with shelters is that the main shelter acts as kind of the middleman. You may go there at first, but once you are in the system, you travel from church to church sleeping in the basement or wherever they have room for you. That means that every week you are shipped off to a new place. I guess the churches just take turns opening their basements to the homeless. So not only did I have to live on a cot in a room full of strangers, but I was also in a new place every single week.

Because we were constantly on the move, we never unpacked the few things we carried with us. We also had to take our belongings with us wherever we went since we might not know from one day to the next where we would be sent. The arrangement was better than living on the street, but it sometimes felt just as unstable and as embarrassing, especially at school.

When you are being moved around constantly, you lose all sense of security. My life was not fixed in any way shape or form. The only constant I had was my school, and that was torture. Before we became homeless, I was made fun of for the way I dressed. Now that we were living in "the shelter," we were carrying our belongings with us to school and we are also picked up and dropped off by a special van just for homeless kids, and everyone at school knew exactly what the plastic bags full of clothes and the van meant.

"You're on the homeless van!" kids would screech as we unloaded in the morning before school.

"Look at all the homeless kids!" I could hear some thoughtless boy yell as we pulled up with all the other buses. "Hey homeless girl! You homeless!" kids would taunt. Talk about a stigmatizing bus ride.

I was so shy that I didn't have any friends at school, so the only time anyone ever talked to me was to ask me if I was homeless or to make fun of me for the way I dressed. We had to get all our clothes from the donation boxes in the shelters, so I was forced to wear whatever I could find, no matter what it looked like or what decade it was from.

"Who wears clothes like that?" a punk kid would ask me before the bell would ring for class to begin.

"What's up with those shoes?" a girl would snicker as she called me out in front of the entire science class. "Are those your grandma's clothes?"

My face would burn with embarrassment as I tried to get to my desk as fast as I could so people would stop laughing at me. And every morning, there was the shelter van to deal with on top of that. Every morning I dreaded getting on that stupid van that might as well have had a sign that said, "LOOK AT ME! I'M POOR!" on the side of it. I had to fight just to make it through the day. I was so distracted with being made fun of that I couldn't focus on my studies. I would cry to my brother, but I didn't share it with my mom because I couldn't put that burden on her. I knew she had enough to fight with herself.

Every morning on the way to school I wanted to disappear into the vinyl seats so I wouldn't have to step down out of the homeless van. I wanted to leave school and never come back. But more than anything else, I wanted to live a normal life where you went home to the same place day after day and you rode the same bus as everyone else. That wasn't my reality though.

Another bad thing about moving every week is that we always had to say goodbye to people. I was painfully shy, but when you live in the same basement with people for seven straight days, sometimes you meet others that you feel a connection with. There is something like a sense of community that happens among everyone, but that was always broken up at the end of the week when it was time to move on to a new place. We were being uprooted every seven days, so there was no sense of stability what-so-ever.

On one occasion there were two little girls I met who made me feel something that few kids my age ever did—they made me feel worthy of friendship.

We were at one of the local churches and these girls were daughters of one of the volunteers who worked in the kitchen. They would come with their mom everyday and play with the kids from the shelter. It was so strange to me to see these little girls, who I imagined were rich and had things like their own bedroom and lacy dresses hanging in their walk-in closets, play with grungy kids like me.

"You want to learn how to play the piano?" they asked me one day when we were all in the recreational room messing around.

"Me?" I asked, almost whispering my question. I couldn't believe they were talking to me.

"Yeah," one of the girls smiled. "We can teach you a song if you want."

"Sure," I said, as I walked over to the piano.

"Here, you can sit between us," one girl said as she scooted over to make room for me.

As I squeezed in between the two girls, my heart felt like it was about to burst. I had not felt that kind of kindness since Mike had sent me the smiley face pizza. I wanted to cry I was so happy in that moment. As the girls showed me which keys to hit and when to hit them, I wanted to hug them and thank them for talking to me. I knew that would seem strange though, so I kept quiet and pushed the keys down as they instructed. I beamed with joy as I sat between those two girls though. Jesus was alive and well in that church recreational room that day.

When I first saw those girls show up at the shelter with their parents, I knew for sure that they wouldn't want anything to do with any of us. We were dirty and poor. We slept on cots at night in the basements of churches. And those girls, they were rich and pretty and clean. When I looked at them, I longed for their lives. I knew for sure that anyone like that wouldn't have something to do with a ratty, homeless girl like me, with my torn pants and my grass-stained Goodwill tennis shoes. They proved me wrong though.

Those two girls were the closest thing I ever had to a friend outside of Paul. That made leaving that church especially hard for me because I knew that once I left, I would never see either of them again. Those girls made me feel like I wasn't lower than everyone else just because of my situation. When they invited me to play the piano or asked me if I wanted to play tag, they weren't just including me in on their playtime; they were teaching me that I was a human being too. Those girls taught me more than just a neat little song on the piano; they taught me that I was a person worthy of friendship and that I wasn't bad because I was poor. When I had to say goodbye to them, it tore me apart. That was just a part of my life, though, so I had to do it and just be happy that I was blessed enough to meet those amazingly kind little girls.

Along with moving constantly and being made fun of for riding the shelter van, another major setback to living at a shelter is that there is zero privacy, which is a real bummer when you are a twelve-year-old girl. I started my period in a church basement and it was near traumatizing. I had to go into the bathroom that I shared with twenty other people and make a makeshift maxi pad out of the cardboard from an empty toilet paper roll and one of my socks. We had no money for anything else and even if we did, I couldn't tell my mom because the whole room would hear me.

Starting your period is a very private thing for a young girl, and it can also be very frightening and even embarrassing. I had a thousand questions and fears about the whole thing, but I had no way of taking my mother aside to ask her any questions or to talk to her about it. I stayed quiet and tried to figure it out on my own, unsure of what all to expect or what to do and how to handle my changing body. It was like a nightmare come true to have that happen in the middle of all that. It was the last thing I wanted to deal with, but there it was.

Becoming a woman while homeless brings with it a host of problems that people who have never experienced being truly poor may even think of. Of course, there was the fact that I was sleeping in a room and sharing a bathroom with dozens of other people, but bigger than that was that when you don't have enough money for clothes, food, or a house, you also don't have enough money for necessary feminine hygiene products. This topic may make some people uncomfortable just to read about, but that is the honest to God truth in the matter and if you think it's uncomfortable to read about it, you should have been there to experience it firsthand.

I have no doubts that the women working in the shelters would have done whatever they could have to help me get what I needed, but I was twelve at the time and I was way too shy and embarrassed to let anyone know that I needed their help. I wanted to conceal it as much as I could, not broadcast it to the world or discuss it with a stranger. So, just as Paul and I had to find creative ways to eat all those evenings that my mom was at work, I had to start finding creative ways to take care of my brand-new problem. My mom did not have any money to give me to go down to the pharmacy, and I was not about to ask anyone for it, so I ended up resorting to empty toilet paper rolls and old socks in place of sanitary napkins on a pretty regular basis. I could just keep washing the socks in the sink and reuse them, so I didn't have to bother my mom or tell anyone.

Since I was in a basement sleeping on church cots and using the bedding that the churches provided for us, I also could hardly sleep at night for fear that I'd wake up in a pool of blood. I didn't have the luxury of simply running my sheets to the laundry room and grabbing some clean ones from the linen closet in the hallway. If I had any kid of accident in the night, then everyone would know—

young, old, woman, and man, everyone would know. And not only that, but I was terrified that the people at the church would get on to me for ruining the sheets. So, after the fateful night that I ran to the bathroom with stomach cramps, I spent seven nights out of every month hardly sleeping and keeping my legs squeezed together as tightly as I could. It was just another thing that reminded me of how awful homelessness was.

It didn't take long for me to decide that I couldn't handle being tossed from church to church, carrying around all my possessions and being made fun of from the time I stepped off the shelter van until the time I finally got back to whatever shelter we were staying in. At the shelter, there were only other homeless kids, so no one could judge me for my family's bad luck. I couldn't figure out how exactly we were going to get out of this place, but I knew that somehow if I just prayed hard enough and trusted God with all I had that we would get out, so that is exactly what I did. Without any reason to believe that things would get better, I prayed every night and talked to God about it, and I believed that God was hearing all I had to say. I also believed that God was going to come through, if only I would keep my faith up. And let me tell you, there were times that it took everything I had not to throw my hands in the air and tell God that I was done—to get so angry and fed up with my lot in life that I just turned my back on everything like so many other people I had seen around the hard neighborhoods we had lived in since I could remember.

Although from the outside looking in, there would be plenty of people who wouldn't have blamed me for giving up all hope or for being consumed with anger, there was still something in me that told me that God was going to get me out of this. That's the thing about faith, I guess. You have it even when the facts tell you there is no reason to. I knew that God was bigger than this though, so I kept my faith and I kept my hope, and that faith paid off, because soon something miraculous happened, but we were pushed to our limits, just like Job was, before that miracle came into our lives.

Chapter Six: End of My Rope

As weeks and months passed in the shelter, slowly Paul and I got a little more used to our new, always-changing way of life. I say we got used to it, but that doesn't necessarily mean that it got any easier for us. It only means that being homeless became less foreign to us and we learned what to expect from day to day. No matter how long you are homeless though, and how accustomed you are to being tossed around and teased, you long for your own home to come home to, a real bed to sleep in at nights, maybe even a few toys that don't have a church's name written on them in magic marker, and some clothes that fit the way they should.

We got used to our schedules though and we learned to adapt to change. We had to be at the shelter by 6pm every evening to be sure we got a place to sleep and made it in time to eat. At the shelter, we gave our names and waited for a van to pick us up and take us to whichever church was on the rotation that week. We'd all pile in the van, our bags in hand, and off we were to the place we'd call home for the next seven days. Once we arrived at the church, it was like the Oklahoma land run of 1889—everyone poured into the basement to stake claim to a cot and set up camp. It was best to avoid the middle area and to keep a safe distance from the bathroom so you didn't have people stumbling into you all night or the sound of the toilet flushing to keep you awake. The last people down to claim their couple of cots would be either right in the middle, where it was near impossible to get up and down if you had to go pee in the middle of the night, or right by the bathroom, where the smell of urine and orange cleaner was the strongest and the traffic was the heaviest.

    The shelter was nothing more than a place we went to be picked up and dropped off; it was more like a bus terminal than it was a temporary home for the homeless. If you have never experienced homelessness firsthand, you may think of a shelter as, well, a shelter—from the elements, from the streets, from being a kid with nowhere to go. That isn't the case at all though. The shelter only opened its doors long enough to get us to a van. That meant that from 6 am to 6 pm when the churches weren't open to us, we were on our own. It's amazing how difficult it is to fill time when you don't have anywhere to go home to.

Because school ended at 3 pm, we had a few hours to kill between the times the last bell rang and the shelter was ready for us. For a kid whose got no home, that is tough. While our classmates were counting down the minutes of the school day so they could get home and play video games or watch after-school cartoons, Paul and I were trying to figure out where we would go that wouldn't kick us out.

Being homeless brings out the resourcefulness in a person. My brother and I figured out that there are some places that are better than others for a couple of kids with no money to spend and hours to kill. We would go to the public library on some days. People are dying to get kids into the library, so that is one place that we knew wouldn't kick us out if we didn't buy anything. Sometimes we would thumb through books or listen to the record players they had for public use. Other times we would just hang out and play games quietly or play hide and seek and hope the librarian didn't catch us zipping through the aisles of books or hiding beneath the desks set up for people to sit and read or write at.

If the library sounded too boring, we would go to the Salesian Boys Club. This was more up Paul's alley because he was a lot more outgoing than I was, and because he had a lot of energy to burn that made the hushed and studious atmosphere of the library hard to handle for him sometimes. A lot of the other kids from the shelter would go there during the day, too. At the boys' club, there was a lot more to do than at the library. We would play ping pong or basketball, and there were always plenty of board games for us. The boys' club was great because you could read or do your homework there if you wanted to, just like at the library, but you could also run around and be a kid.

If we ever found spare change anywhere, Paul and I would spend our time waiting for six to roll around at a couple of the nearby fast food restaurants. The ones with the playgrounds were the best, because there is only so much time you can spend sitting in a hard, plastic chair in a freezing cold restaurant listening to elevator music. The restaurants with playgrounds we could go to even if we didn't have enough money to buy an apple pie of an ice cream cone, and the managers hardly ever paid attention to us as long as we didn't cause any trouble.

What was different about going to a fast food restaurant was it seemed that going to those places reminded me more that Paul and I didn't get to experience childhood like so many other kids did. While Paul was busy spinning himself sick on one of the playground toys, I'd sit and watch as a mom still dressed in her slacks and silk blouse from work come in with her two children. I'd see them go up to the register and Mom would ask her two kids what they wanted. Each would be tugging at either side of their mom, hopping up and down and excitedly shouting out their dinner requests.

"I want a cheeseburger!" one would beg.

"I want nuggets!" the other would crowd in on top of his sister. "With honey!"

"A cheeseburger for you and chicken nuggets for you?" Mom would ask looking down at her son and daughter. "You're both sure?"

"Yeah!" the two would cry out in unison.

I couldn't ever remember Paul and I being as carefree or happy as those two kids. I couldn't ever remember my own mom having the same kind of smile as the mom I watched keep a hand on each of the tops of her children's heads as they waited in line. She would glance down every minute or so and grin, moving her hand to a shoulder or pulling her kids closer to her. It seemed as far away as a fairytale to me to watch these kids with their moms. I would go on to imagine them getting into their nice car and going home to watch a movie together as they waited for their dad to get home from working late that night. I saw them taking bubble baths and splashing wildly in the bathtub as they sank army ships or helped their unicorns save troll dolls from an underwater monster. I watched them as both their parents tucked them into their own beds in their own rooms where a nightlight threw colored stars on the ceiling. I wondered if those kids realized how lucky they were for all those things.

"Paula, look!" Paul would call out from the top of a slide, shaking me out of my thoughts. "I'm on top of the world!"

Maybe some day we will be, I'd think as I stared up at my smiling brother.

Luckily on weekends we were allowed to stay at the shelter twenty-four hours. I suppose they knew that it wouldn't be easy for parents or kids to find something to do for twelve hours when none of us had any money, so they let us stay all day every Saturday and Sunday if we needed to, which we always did. We would sometimes venture out to a playground on Saturdays, and we always had church on Sundays, but other than that, we spent much of our weekends bored to death in the shelter.

Every day, every week was the same thing. We took our plastic trash bags with our belongings everywhere we went. If people couldn't tell we were struggling by our hand-me-down sneakers and our T shirts that were often a size or two too big, then our plastic discount store sacks of clothes were a dead giveaway that we were a tribe of urban Nomads, and the embarrassment of that never wore off.

Something else that never wore off was the pain I felt when I would hear my mom whimpering as everyone around us snored or hacked in their sleep.

Sharing cots and living with sick people was hard enough, but hearing my mom cry every night is what really got to me. I had heard it even when we had our own place. I know my mom wanted more for us when we were living in the insect-infested apartments, surrounded by drug dealers and gang-bangers. Now though, she couldn't even provide us with that, and so she continued to weep—only now she tried to be quiet when she cried, but I could always hear her, and it cut me to the quick.

Hearing my mom crying at night when she thought we were asleep, that was rough. As I lay quietly beside her in my own cot and listened as she sniffed and sobbed, I remember feeling so different. All the other kids that I saw everyday—the kids that teased me and mocked me for my clothes—were sleeping in real beds after an evening of watching sitcoms and doing homework at their kitchen tables. For me it was different altogether. While other kids were lying in bed thinking about how to beat the next level on their video game or dreaming about a boy they had a crush on, I was listening to my mom choke back her tears and wondering what kind of church we'd be in next. I was wondering how soft the cots would be and if the sheets would smell like mildew or bleach. That was my reality. I didn't have a TV to go home and watch. I dug through boxes of clothes in church corners, not clothing racks at department stores to find my clothes and the kids at school who enjoyed the privilege of sharing a bathroom only with their own family didn't go easy on me about that fact either. They reminded me that this was my reality everyday, and I thought about it every night.

Sometimes as I lay quiet and still in the dark of a church basement with the sound of my mom's sobs pounding in my brain, I would cry too. I would bury my face in the pillow the church had provided for me and I would cry with my mom. I cried for her; I cried for Paul; I cried for me; I cried for all the other kids, single moms, ill elderly folks, and social outcasts who dozed and dreamt big dreams of escaping this hell all around me. I also cried out to God.

"Why God? Why are you letting all this happen to us?" I'd whisper into my coarse pillowcase. "What did we do to deserve all this?" I'd ask, and then I would feel anger and frustration drown out the feeling of sadness.

"Why's my daddy get to go around doing whatever he wants, living in his own house and driving around in his own car, and we're in a church basement toting our clothes around in plastic bags, God" I'd demand. "Why don't you just let me die if this is what you have planned for me? I shouldn't even have been brought in this world if you were just going to let me struggle like this. Just take me out of it, God. I've had all I can take!"

I'd fall asleep giving God a piece of my mind. I would have fitful dreams of defending myself at school. I'd wake up with my heart pounding after having dreamt that I came face-to-face with my dad and finally told him how I felt. And sometimes I'd feel bad about what I'd said to God the night before. I would apologize for having slipped in my faith, ask for forgiveness for being mad at my own dad, and remind myself that God would take care of me. I wasn't sure though how much longer I could hang on to that belief.

Every Sunday morning, I was in church wearing my knees out praying to God. I would feel like maybe I was finally getting to him, but then the next week would roll around and steal every bit of optimism and faith that I had. The women in the church would tell me to be strong and just trust the Lord, and the pastor would remind me, "Blessed are the meek, for they shall inherit the earth." When you are twelve and living in damp basements—correction, when you are at any point in your life and living in damp basements—it gets hard to keep your eyes forward and to believe that the meek will inherit anything but heartache. That's where I was—right at the end of my rope. And then an unlikely sports hero showed up out of nowhere and he reminded me that God works in his own time, and that He shows up out of the blue just when you think that He must have forgotten about you.

Chapter Seven: The Letter

February 11, 1990, started out to be an average day for millions of people. But for the boxing world it would be one that they would not soon forget. What may be arguably one of the biggest upsets in boxing history, James "Buster" Douglas knocked out "Iron" Mike Tyson in Tokyo, Japan. That knock-out was 'the fight' that earned Buster Douglas the title of Boxing World Champion. This was just months before my family and I became homeless.

While Buster Douglas was busy answering reporters' questions and posing for pictures that would appear in sports magazines, halfway around the world in Columbus, Ohio there was me and my family, which were in a very different position in life. There were no lights, no glamour, no cameras or news journalists; there was just a little girl with her family trying to sustain their living doing the best they could one day at a time. While a momentous event in boxing history had just taken place, I was preoccupied with more pressing matters—like surviving. Who won the title that year didn't seem to concern me one way or another. All I cared about was dinner. So, the Heavyweight Champ of the World was at his apex, while my struggling family was coming on rock bottom real fast, and for about a year, neither would think anything about the existence of the other. But that would all change in due time.

We'd been basement hopping for months when one day we were at the Salesian Boys Club, which was right around the corner from the shelter. It was a popular place for the kids from the shelter to go while we all waited for the shelter to open. We'd go there to play and do different activities they had there at the club. This day was just like any other. It was about fifteen until four and I was in the middle of a heated ping pong game with Paul when we both suddenly hit with something that felt like electricity in the air.

Paul swiped the ping pong ball out of the air after my serve and stopped right in the middle of our game. We both stood and turned our heads toward a large group of kids who were all chattering on top of one another with excitement.

"What's going on?" I asked Paul. He shrugged his shoulders and we both sat our paddles down on the table and walked over to the crowd.

I went to one of the kids and asked, "Hey, what's going on?"

"Buster Douglas is here!" a short, twiggy kid gasped with excitement.

I didn't know too much about boxing, but I did know that this Buster Douglas was a big deal. This was, after all, after he had won the championship fight. This guy was the undisputed champion. I may not have seen the fight, because we didn't have a television to watch it on at the time, but I had heard his name and seen things in the newspapers about him. When he had won the title, he had been featured in the local paper, *The Columbus Dispatch*, and the whole city was ecstatic about his victory. So, while I was no boxing buff, I knew that Buster Douglas being at the boys' club was important. I just didn't know how important it would be for me personally.

So, after the boy with the matchstick arms told me what all the commotion was about, I decided that I had better not let my chance at seeing a real boxing legend pass me by, no matter how much I did or didn't know about boxing. I pushed my way through the screaming boys and girls and got up to a window. I cupped my hand and pressed them to the glass so I could get a good look, and there he was— it was Mr. Douglas himself, and he was there with his son. I never realized how much I wanted to meet a sports hero until that day I saw Buster, but there was security all around him and no way I was going to get close enough to him to meet him. They were shooting a commercial at the Salesian Boys and Girls club that day, so he would probably just come and go, and that would be the end of that.

I slumped back from the window for a minute, and then I felt a surge of excitement swell in my belly and shoot through my body. Maybe I won't get to meet him, I thought, but I bet my mom would at least like to see him in person. It wasn't everyday we got a chance to be so close to someone so famous. This could be the highlight of my mom's otherwise darkest year. I darted out of the crowd and ran downstairs to the receptionist's office.

"Can you call my mom, please?" I panted anxiously. "I want to tell her about Buster Douglas!"

"Sure thing," the receptionist smiled. "What's the number?"

"She's at the shelter," I wheezed. I tried to get a hold of myself. I was so excited I would nearly feel my head floating away from my body.

"Here you are," the receptionist said as she handed me the receiver and finished dialing. As soon as someone picked up, I blurted out my mom's name and said it was an emergency. I imagine the person on the other end assumed someone was on fire the way I was talking.

"Paula?" my mom said as she picked up the phone. "What is going on?"

"Momma, Buster Douglas is here! At the club, Momma! I saw him," I yelled into the phone, barely getting the words out of my mouth.

"Wow, oh my God!" my mom replied. "You should get his autograph. It's not everyday you get to meet someone like him."

"Do you wanna come see him?"

"Paula, I won't be able to make it," she told me. "But you go try."

"I better go, Mom," I said, realizing Buster could leave before I got off the phone and I'd lose my chance. "I'm gonna try to meet him."

I got an idea while I was talking to my mom on the phone. I had decided when I was standing there earlier staring at him through a window that there was too much commotion and security around him to meet him, but talking to my mom inspired me to at least write him a letter to tell him my story. After all, I had nothing to lose from trying. And I wasn't going to just try to get an autograph. I was going to tell Buster about my family. Maybe this was the moment I'd been waiting for since we showed up at the shelter months before. Maybe this wasn't just a boxer showing up to do a commercial; maybe this was an answer to a really big prayer.

"Do you have a piece of paper and a pen I could borrow?" I asked the receptionist as I handed her the phone receiver.

"I bet I do," she said as she hung up the phone and swiveled her chair to face the back part of her desk. "Here you go!" she said, handing over a piece of printer paper and a ballpoint pen.

"Thank you so much," I said to the receptionist, and then I sat down and wrote the following letter to Buster Douglas:

Dear Buster Douglas,

My name is Paula Taylor. Me and my family is homeless. We live in the Faith Mission Shelter. Can you please come to help us? Please come and show us that you care about our community.

Thank you,

Paula Taylor

After writing the letter, I put my right hand on it and said, "Father, let every word of this letter touch Buster's heart, in Jesus' name I pray, amen."

I handed the receptionist her pen, thanked her again, and ran off to get my note to Buster. I had written the note with all the confidence in the world, but as I made my way back upstairs, I started to get extremely nervous. I began to second-guess myself and I even got scared about how I would get the letter to the boxer. I was painfully shy, and this was a big deal. How in the world was I going to walk up to a famous athlete and deliver a letter asking for his help? I felt my limbs turn to mashed potatoes and my chest squeeze my lungs. I just couldn't do it. But then I thought of someone who probably could—Paul! Unlike me, my brother was rambunctious and outgoing. He wasn't too shy to do anything, so instead of going to Buster, I went straight to Paul.

"Paul," I said as I tugged at his shirt. "Paul, I need you to do something."

"What?" he asked as he whirled around to face me.

"I wrote this letter for Buster and I'm too scared to give it to him. It's about helping us though, and I want him to read it."

"Shoot, I'll take it," he said with a grin as he held out his hand to take the letter.

I held the letter out to him, and as Paul took off for Buster, I mustered up enough courage to follow behind him to watch as he delivered what would be the most important letter of my life. I tried to stay as hidden as I could, and when Paul got closer, I peeled away from him and disappeared in a group of kids. I peeked from behind a shorter girl with crazy hair to see if he was going to go through with it. Sure enough, Paul walked right up to a security guard and handed him the folded-up piece of paper.

"This is a letter my little sister wrote for Buster," he said confidently. "Can you give it to him?"

"The security guard looked at Paul with some amusement and at the letter this spunky kid was holding in his hand. He finally took the letter and said, "Yes I will."

As I watched the bulky man with the smooth, bald head in the blue uniform take the tiny piece of paper from my brother, I was bombarded with too many thoughts to keep up with. Doubt and fear gnawed at me and taunted me, telling me that he wasn't going to get the letter. He doesn't have time for a homeless girl, my insecurities mocked. I tried to push those negative thoughts out of my brain and let whatever would happen, happen. *God's got it now*, I told myself.

After Paul delivered the letter, we went back to the shelter and I went on about my business. I tried to forget about the letter altogether. I didn't want to listen to all the doubts anymore, and I also didn't want to get my hopes up. I had given it a try; that was all I could do.

Night settled down on Columbus, and I went through the same routine as always. Only this time, I felt like something was a little different. Nights were usually pretty glum in the shelters and church basements. It was at night that all the troubles of the world seemed to sneak up from the concrete floors to bully you while you tried to get comfortable on your cot. It was at night when you were left alone in the dark quiet with only your thoughts, and when you are homeless, that can be a scary and depressing time. This night was different though.

This night I felt something I had never felt in the basement of a church: I felt hope, and I felt excited. As much as I didn't want to get my hopes up, I couldn't help feeling a new kind of optimism creep in. I liked the feeling. I imagine it is the same feeling other kids got the night before their birthdays or Christmas mornings. Even if I would be disappointed in the long run, it was worth that one night of hope. I fell asleep that night smiling, and I dreamt of a boxer who lifted me up on his shoulders, up toward heaven. It was the most peaceful dream I could remember having.

The next day I woke up, and I was snapped back to reality. There was a line to use the bathroom, a line to get breakfast, and I had to put my dingy, worn out tennis shoes on with my pants and shirt that looked like they had snuck out of the closet of a colorblind school teacher two decades before. I went to school, and the optimism that I had the night before was still there, but I could feel it fading. Every time I heard the crackling of the intercom, excitement stirred in my chest. I waited for my name to be called. I waited for everyone to rush to watch me as I went to the office to meet Buster. I was disappointed four times that day by the morning announcements, by Dwayne Johnson being called out for a dentist appointment, by the announcement that we are not to put gum in the water fountains, and by the assistant principal accidently buzzing my classroom. My heart sunk a little lower every time the announcement wasn't for me.

The next day was no different. I fell asleep the night before with a little seed of hope budding in my heart, and that seedling wilted a little each hour that went by when I heard nothing in response to my letter. I knew it was a long shot, but I really thought that maybe Buster was my guardian angel, sent to help my family finally get out of the rut we had been in for so long. I started to scold myself for being so silly. Why in the world would Buster care about me and my family, anyway?

Chapter Eight: The Heavyweight Champ

A few days passed, and I had nearly resigned to my fate. I knew that it was crazy to think that handing a champion boxer a letter would turn everything around for me and my family. On day three of hearing nothing, like always I got to the shelter when it opened for the evening and sat down to work on some math homework. I noticed the center director walking toward me before I could even get settled.

"Someone special came here to see you," Mr. Lee, the shelter director, said to me.

I looked up at him a little confused. I knew it wasn't my dad coming back to claim me, and I didn't know anyone else who would show up at the shelter to visit with me. I didn't have any friends and Mr. Lee wouldn't call my mom a special visitor. A quick list of possibilities ran through my head, but none of them made any sense. Before I could ask who though, Mr. Lee told me.

"It was James 'Buster' Douglas," he said, his eyes shining and his lips curling into the biggest smile I'd ever seen. "He asked for you. He came here just to talk to you, but you weren't in."

My heart broke right in two. I wished I wouldn't have even heard he'd been there. It was like I had gotten a winning lottery ticket and then accidently thrown it out the window. I could have almost thrown up I was so upset.

"Don't worry," Mr. Lee assured me. "He'll be back."

All I could think about was, 'He's not coming back. He too busy. He had already taken time out to come and I wasn't here.'

But as fate would have it, Buster did come back the following day, but I was gone again. Mr. Lee came to me again once I arrived and told me about it.

"He came by and donated a bunch of supplies and food for the shelter," Mr. Lee explained, "But he was here for you again."

This time I started crying. I couldn't believe how much bad luck I had. Even when it looked like I was finally having good luck, there was my dreaded foe, disappointment, following me around to ruin everything. All I could think was that since I missed him a second time that I'd never see him. I was sure that he wouldn't come back a third time. Even if he wanted to, a guy like him didn't have the time to keep coming back to a shelter to see some little girl.

"Don't get upset," Mr. Lee comforted me. "I'm sure he'll be back. He came back once. Why not again?"

I didn't say anything back to Mr. Lee. I looked up and nodded to him to let him know that I appreciated his kind words. Then I walked off to cry some more about my near brush with a miracle. It was like life just wanted to keep me down.

The weekend came and went and I didn't feel any better about missing Buster Douglas not once, but twice. I was devastated. I had the golden ticket in my hand and I just let it go. I was beating myself up over it. I felt like I hadn't just let myself down, but I had let my entire family down. I could've gotten us out of there, but now all that was gone.

"Paula, you cannot keep beating yourself up," my mom told me. "You didn't let anyone down. If Buster Douglas wanted to do something, he would do it whether he met you or not. There's no use thinking you could have changed anything."

"He asked to talk to me though, mom," I sobbed. "And I wasn't there."

"Well, these things happen. And you know what, Paula?" she asked me, pulling my face up so I was looking at her. "You tried and that is all that matters."

"I just wanted to save us," I cried.

"That's my job," my mom told me. "You shouldn't even be thinking like that."

I tried to let it go and not feel like I'd let everyone down. Buster did donate a lot to the shelter, which did help a lot. And there was no way for me to know that he'd show up when he did. I wanted to believe I hadn't thrown away our chance at a normal life, but I just couldn't fully convince myself. It really did feel worse than never having hope to begin with. It felt like a cruel joke to have the idea of a better life dangled in front of your nose and then just ripped away. Again, I felt like Job as he watched his house crumble and his livestock drop dead. I was just like Job, and soon I would find out that was truer than I could ever imagine.

The week after I had missed Buster Douglas two times, I was in history class when my assistant principal, Mr. Glover, knocked on the door.

"Sorry to interrupt," he said as he poked his head in the classroom. "But I need Paula Taylor, please."

My heart skipped a beat when I heard my name. This was strange because, one, I hadn't done anything to have to go to the principal's office, and two, kids were usually called to the office over the intercom. I could feel the blood rush to my face as I looked at the assistant principal. I closed my book and put it in my desk as I slid out into the aisle. He gestured to me across the room to follow him into the hallway, and so I did.

"Miss Taylor, you need to come with me to the office," he said once we were both standing in the hallway with the classroom door closed behind us.

"What did I do?" I asked.

Mr. Glover didn't answer my question. He just kept on walking toward the principal's office. I figured his silence was not a good sign for me, but there was nothing I could think of that I'd be in hot water for. I was chewing gum in class earlier that day, but surely, I wouldn't be taken out of class for that.

I made it through dead mans' walk with my stoically quiet vice principal. By the time we got to the office, I was about to explode in anticipation. I felt I was being taken to a firing squad, but I hadn't been given a fair trial. That was just my luck, though.

We got to the office and Mr. Glover reached to open the door for me. As the door swung open, there stood the six-foot four-inch, 231-pound heavyweight boxing champion of the world. Everything froze—the scene, my mind, my tongue. I couldn't even blink to make sure that what I was seeing was real. I could not believe this. James "Buster" Douglas was standing in my school.

"Are you Paula?" Buster asked as I stood stunned in the doorway.

I shook my head yes. And as I stood there, not being able to speak, I stared right at him and I saw tears well up in his eyes. I realized in that moment that the Heavyweight Champ of the World was relieved to have found me, a little homeless girl from Columbus, Ohio. He was just as excited to meet me as I was to meet him. Just thinking about someone as important as him tracking me down overwhelmed me. And suddenly I had tears in my eyes, too.

"Do you mind going to the next room so I can talk to you in private?" he asked. I nodded and we went into a conference room to talk.

"I got your letter, Paula," he told me. "And I plan to do whatever I can to help your family."

"Thank you," I managed to get out. "Thank you so much."

"You deserve it, Paula," he told me. "I want to know what I can do to get your family back on their feet," he went on. "And I plan on making sure that you never have to sleep in a shelter again."

"I knew God would answer my prayers," was the thought that kept running in my head. "I just knew that He would."

"My mom and brother aren't gonna believe this," I said. I could hardly believe it myself.

"I plan on meeting them too," Buster told me. "I need to talk to your mom to see what we can do to get to guys in a house."

"A house?" I asked to make sure I heard him right.

"Yes," he smiled.

"I can't believe this is happening," I muttered. "Thank you so much," I repeated. I couldn't say thank you enough to this man who had just walked into my life and was going to change everything when he didn't even know me.

"We all need a little help sometimes," he told me.

We talked a little longer and I explained how my family had come to live in church basements. I also told him about how Paul and I had to steal to eat sometimes, as ashamed as I was.

"You don't need to be ashamed," he told me. "People have to eat. But I want to make sure you never have to steal again."

Once we finished up talking, we made plans for Buster to meet my family, which he did.

A few days later he showed up at the place we were staying at around two in the morning. I figured he came at that time to avoid any attention unto himself. He came in and met my mom and brother. Of course, Paul had no problems gabbing away at the boxing champion. My mom, on the other hand, was also excited and grateful in meeting the champ. She could only say thank you over and over to Buster as he sat with us and talked about how he would help us out in any way that he could.

From that day on, I established a relationship with James Buster Douglas that was the closest thing I ever had to a healthy father-daughter relationship.

I remember going to his Florida house for the summers and Christmas breaks. I would babysit his boys and hang out with his wife.

One of the great memories I have also was going to Las Vegas to visit. What a beautiful place. That was the first time I was able to have crab legs and a virgin strawberry daiquiri all to myself. While staying at the Mirage, they took me to get my hair done and that too was the first time I went to a professional hair salon.

Buster became a part of my family, and I became a part of his. He and his wife were instrumental in my development as a teenager. They paid for my driving lessons, my braces, and my college tuition and helped my family and me a great deal so we would never have to sleep on cots or go without dinner to keep the lights on ever again. God's favor fell on my life in an unexplainable way.

They bought my mom a van which was a miracle in itself. Now we wouldn't have to wait around in the freezing snow or rain at the bus stops since we didn't own a car. God's favor fell on my life in an unexplainable way.

Not too long after we met Buster, my mom finally found a job. She got an apartment that she could afford and with Buster's help from time to time, we were always able to make ends meet. I didn't have to steal clothes or sell candy to eat anymore, and I even went on to college. I went from being a homeless little girl with no hope who couldn't stand going to school, to college. That is nothing short of a God thing.

My life took a dramatic shift in ways I could not have ever imagined. There is a verse in the Bible from Ephesians 3:20 that says, *"Now to Him who is able to do exceedingly abundantly above all that we ask or think, according to the power that works in us, to Him be glory in the church by Christ Jesus to all generations, forever and ever. Amen."*

That verse literally became alive in my life. God more than exceeded my expectations of what I asked or thought. The little mustard seed of faith I had was swelling up in my little spirit and I saw God intervene in a most miraculous way.

What a mighty God we serve. I look back now, and I can see very clearly the parallels of my life to that of Job's. And in the end, God gave me more than double for my trouble. I could have never guessed when we received that eviction notice after my mom lost her job that one day a boxing champion would show up at my school and change my life forever, but that's just how God is. He really does work in mysterious ways, and that is something that I remind myself every time life hits me with hardship—God has a bigger plan; I just need to trust that everything will come into place when the timing is right.

Chapter Nine: ...but joy comes in the morning

When I laid my hands on that letter and prayed, *"Father, let every word of this letter touch Buster's heart, in Jesus' name I pray, amen."*, God made sure that my prayer was heard specifically to what I asked him. I say that because shortly after meeting Buster, the Columbus Dispatch had a picture of Buster and I as the headline read, *"Twelve-year old's letter tugs at heartstrings of boxing champion."* God let me know that he heard my prayer in the exact way I prayed it.

What Buster Douglas did for me was a gift that kept on giving. I mentioned that he paid my way through college, and it was at World Harvest Bible College (now renamed Valor Christian College) in Canal Winchester, OH, that I met my husband. I know that I would never have found a man fit for me if I hadn't been in the environment I was in.

You see, because of what happened to me when I was just four years old, coupled with the fact I never had a father figure in my life, I had a real problem with men—I didn't know how to be affectionate or in a relationship. In fact, I had never been in a relationship until my husband. The fact that I was so standoffish with the opposite sex, no man was ever interested in getting to know me, nor was I ever interested in a man. Because my husband was a godly man, however, he had the patience that I needed to come out of my shell and learn to love.

When I think of how hard it must've been for my husband the first several years with me my heart swells with gratitude. I was so emotionally stunted that I wouldn't even hold his hand for some time. And any time he went to hug me, I cowered from him or stiffened when his arm touched me. Forget about a kiss. My husband was dedicated and loving while he waited though. He let me move at my own pace and he showed me what real unconditional love was. Watching him love me, I learned how to love him back. I always knew from the time I met him that I wanted to be with him, I just didn't have the tools to be in a relationship. He helped me get those tools though. And where typical college men may spend all their time trying to get a girl in bed, my husband spent praying for me. He showed me that I could trust a man. It wasn't without its challenges. He grew more and more as a man throughout our relationship and I did the same as a woman.

We were both virgins when we got together and remained that way until our wedding day. Today I am married to that amazing man and I have three kids of my own. I thank God everyday that they have a mother and father to grow up with and that their father is the loving, godly man that he is. I know that, even if we sometimes cannot provide monetarily in the way we would like, that my children always know that they are loved and that they can trust both their parents with anything. I think that is vital for any child.

We just celebrated 21 years of marriage. Sometimes I can't believe that it has been that long already. One day my husband and I will have to write about our journey.

My adulthood came with many challenges but the faith that grew inside of me as a result of what God did for me with Buster allowed me to handle those difficulties knowing that the power of God's grace was over my life.

In 2010, when we faced foreclosure from my husband being laid off a couple years prior, we felt the call of God to start a ministry. The following seven years was a time where God restored, molded, and strengthened us preparing us for ministry. We started having services in our home in January 2017 and we launched our church plant in March 2018.

We now pastor Harmony Church in Columbus, Ohio and are walking this new chapter in our lives. God has blessed us with our home in Pickerington, OH. Our boys are serving God and fulfilling their destiny.

My husband and I couldn't be prouder of our boys. The faithfulness of God in our lives has made an impact in them to have a solid foundation of their conviction.

As far as my father, I am very proud of what God has done in his life. He has since dedicated his life to the Lord. What an awesome and loving God we serve. Whenever I visit my hometown of Akron,

I have the chance to see him. He is in ministry also and is serving the Lord in his community.

You see, God has a knack for taking the unqualified underdog and making them into His conquering warriors.

So, wherever you are in this journey called life, don't lose hope. I know firsthand the feelings of hopelessness, but understand that nothing surprises God. He is in control of it all. My story is one that may seem extraordinary, but know that God is not limited in His capabilities. Your story is going to be different than mine. Perhaps you may be facing a hard and difficult time in your life as you read this. Maybe you are facing a divorce, or the loss of a loved one, or on the verge of losing your home; whatever it is, don't lose hope. Stir up your faith and ask God for His divine intervention. You never know what He will do unless you ask in faith.

We all live a life that at times is vulnerable in different seasons. I have navigated different seasons where I have had to remind myself that this is a journey of faith.

And while I feel overwhelmed at times and I have no idea how somethings will play out, I do know that some day I will be looking back at that part of my life and I will say, "God brought me through that and I am better for it," just like the way I look back at my childhood and am reminded, "God brought me through that and I am better for it." I just have to keep looking forward and know that God is faithful. I have to know that there is something bigger around the bend, and that even if I don't get why God is letting things happen the way He is, that there is a reason.

Let that be your mindset, your belief. That God is faithful and that He won't abandon you. If you are going through something that is overwhelming right now, let me say this prayer for you,

"Dear heavenly Father, I pray for the individual reading this book right now. I ask that you may breathe life, hope, and joy into their hearts. Reveal who you are to them. Let them experience a supernatural touch from the Holy Spirit. In Jesus' name, Amen."

Now, on the other hand, if you are someone who is living an extremely blessed life, my prayer is that you can be the answer to someone else's prayer. Be generous, be giving, be thoughtful and perform an act of kindness like Buster did for me. I promise you, you will reap big dividends of that kindness in ways you never expected.

    I leave you with this—sometimes things happen to people that makes no sense at all. Terrible people stumble onto fortunes that they don't deserve nor will they ever do anything good with, and amazing people with amazing hearts are dealt one bad hand after the next. But at the same time, miracles happen all the time, and amazing people show compassion to those who need it most, the way Buster did for my family. So, when it feels like your world is being swept away, try to remember that you will survive, and to look for all the miracles in life instead of focusing on the negative things. If I wouldn't have believed in miracles, I would've never written that letter to Buster Douglas that day. A little bit of faith can go a very long way. I am living proof of that.

Acknowledgments

I would like to thank my husband and children first and foremost for standing beside me while I worked to get this book completed. A special thanks to my husband, who is my rock.

Of course, I would like to recognize James "Buster" Douglas, without whom there would be no story to tell. What you did for my family was like a fairy tale story that came true. Thank you so much.

Finally, I would like to thank Cassandra Woody, whose guidance and skill helped me not only write this book, but to make it all it could be, and whose encouragement helped me believe in myself and my story.

Finally, I must thank God, who I know always has a plan for me, even when I cannot see it, and who is always faithful.

Contact Us;

Paula Penha has been in ministry for over 25 years. She has helped in worship teams and youth groups of various churches she served under. She now serves as a minstrel and is the worship director at Harmony Church where she co-pastor with her husband, Claudio Penha.

She has been married for 21 years and loves being a wife and a mother to her sons.

You can follow them on Instagram

@paula.t.penha

@claudio.a.penha

@myharmony.church

www.ingramcontent.com/pod-product-compliance
Lightning Source LLC
Chambersburg PA
CBHW031559040426
42452CB00006B/356